"If all you can do is crawl, start crawling."

—Rumi

"It is in your hands to create a better world
for all who live in it."

—Nelson Mandela

DICTIONARY FOR A BETTER WORLD

POEMS, QUOTES, and ANECDOTES from A to Z

Irene Latham & Charles Waters

Illustrated by **Mehrdokht Amini**

🐚 CAROLRHODA BOOKS
MINNEAPOLIS

CONTENTS

Irene Latham wrote the poems with **red** titles. Charles Waters wrote the poems with **blue** titles. The poets jointly wrote the poems with **purple** titles.

WORDS FOR A BETTER WORLD

Awash in attempts to help cool our fevered world, we

Begin simply with words. We savor syllables,

Consider history and meaning. We forge ahead with

Determination, trying to do what's right, though

Each step is filled with uncertainty.

For what is more powerful—more dangerous—than words? What

Gathers us, divides us like these letters and how we arrange them?

How can we use words to improve ourselves and inspire *Mindfulness*

In the hearts of others without perpetuating fears, misunderstandings?

"Just try," a small voice whispers. So we listen and share. We ponder

Karma and *Courage, Tenacity,* and *Hope.* We unspool our

Lives, remembering triumphs and failures. We write—

Making poems that celebrate *Acceptance, Freedom, Respect,* building each

Necessary step to show more *Compassion* and *Gratitude.*

Our stories put a spotlight on making friends—and losing them. About

Past mistakes and what we're learning. In this never-ending

Quest to change the world, we challenge ourselves with new forms:

Roundel, cherita, limerick, shadorma. We abandon our complacency,

Search within ourselves for how to be changemakers, not

Thinking we have all the answers. Now we listen to opposing views with an *Open* spirit.

Understanding takes time. We must be patient as our new

Vocabulary takes root, trusting that change will one day bloom.

We're unsure, yet willing to bring our authentic selves to you, not some

Xeroxed copy of who we wish to be. This is our moment. Please join us—

You can start with any word you choose. Read with *Empathy* and *Zest.*

Zoom into each new moment ready to bring your best self to the world.

Abecedarian: each line or stanza begins with the first letter of the alphabet and continues with letters in successive order

ACCEPTANCE

I am a word with teeth—
a crocodile
sunning on a muddy bank.

Some fear me;
others misunderstand me.

Yet I do not flounder (as you do)
in that unhappy swamp
between the way things are

and the way I'd like
them to be.

I rest in what is—
drowsy, still—
belly bulging

as a plover picks bits
of meat from my mouth.

Persona: written in the voice of
the subject of the poem

> "Do we dare be ourselves?
> That is the question that counts."
> —Pablo Casals

IRENE SAYS . . .

For many years I thought "acceptance" was some sort of giving in—a weakness. I've believed strongly in my own power to change things, to create the life I want. But what about the things I can't change? Acceptance is actually coming to peace with those things, which takes tremendous courage. I can't change other people. I can only change me. And instead of beating myself up for not being more social, more outspoken, more forgiving, more whatever—the best thing I can do is accept myself right where I am at this very moment. Because like that drowsy crocodile, where I am—and where you are—is exactly where you need to be.

TRY IT!

Today give yourself—and those around you—a break. Allow everyone to be where they are. Come back to this book tomorrow and the next day and the next. See what happens!

ALLY

Take one cup of understanding:
When you listened,
without interruption,
after I explained
why a joke you made
about my faith wasn't
funny to me, then
apologized afterwards.

Two dollops of fortitude:
When you stood next to me
when a pack of bullies
made fun of my complexion,
staring at them so fiercely
I thought each of them
would dissolve until one by one
they walked away, defeated.

Three pinches of support:
When you were the only friend to show
up at my first solo piano recital.
Afterwards, my no-nonsense
mother said, "You should invite him
over for dinner sometime."

Stir and marinate:
When you did each of these things
I realized this unbreakable, unshakable
support is the vital ingredient
in a wholehearted ally.

List: a list or inventory of items, people, places, or ideas

"The first thing we need allies to do is listen. Come to us with a willingness to grow and evolve. You're going to make mistakes, and that's fine, but be willing to listen and grow from those mistakes. I think that's the most important trait an ally can have."

—Sarah McBride

CHARLES SAYS . . .

I don't have many friends, yet the ones I do have time and again come through for me. My college professor Jane "Tinker" Foderaro was one of these humans. When I was figuring out how to navigate the world after college graduation, her conversations with me about life, professionalism, and hard work helped me find my way in this glorious, complicated world. I soaked up her suggestions and did my best to apply them to my own life. She took the time to listen, dispense advice, and believe in me. Now I do my best to be an ally as well, and I hope you can too.

TRY IT!

Is there a friend, acquaintance, or someone you may only know a little who supported you during a time of crisis in your life? Use the knowledge they gave you and be the same kind of ally to someone else.

BELONGING

When I walk into the room,
all I want is to fit in.
Can new friendships bloom?
How do I begin?

All I want is to fit in
with this fresh group of friends.
I know it can't begin
until someone bends.

Dear fresh group of friends:
how about you be you, and I'll be me?
When someone bends—
that's the key.

Yes, you be you, and I'll be me,
and new friendships will bloom.
I turn the key.
I walk into the room.

Pantoum: a series of quatrains, with the second and fourth lines of each quatrain repeated as the first and third lines of the next. The second and fourth stanza repeat the first and third lines of the first stanza, but in the opposite order (ending with the first line of the poem).

"If we have no peace, it is because we have forgotten that we belong to each other."

—Mother Teresa

IRENE SAYS . . .

My family moved a lot while I was growing up, so I was far too often walking into a new town, new school, new room. The year we moved to Folsom, Louisiana, it was the middle of the school year, and I was particularly terrified. That's when my mother suggested we have a "new kid party." Before we left our old town in Tennessee, she got all the names of my new classmates from my soon-to-be teacher. In between packing and unpacking boxes, I wrote out invitations to a party at our new house. When the day came for me to walk into that new room, having those invitations in my backpack made it a whole lot easier—although standing in front of the class and reading the names off one by one remains one of the scariest things I have ever done. By the time we actually had the party the following week, friendships had already started to bloom.

TRY IT!

How would your life change—how would YOU change—if you reached out to someone today? No matter our differences, we all have more in common than not. Smile at someone new today, make them feel welcome, important, and valuable.

COMPASSION

Pink light
winks through
blue curtains,

house silent,
save Mama's
hacking—

so I leap up,
wake-dress-feed
my sister.

Together,
we steep Mama
in hugs and blankets,

whisper-sing,
we love you!
feel better!

then walk to the bus stop,
holding hands
the whole way.

Aubade: a morning song

14

"We do not need to understand to feel the pain of another. We do not need to understand to share the joy of another. There is nothing we need to understand to be compassionate with each other."

—Julius Lester, *This Strange New Feeling: Three Love Stories from Black History*

IRENE SAYS . . .

I'm a word person, so the nuances and differences between words matter to me. And for many years I thought of "compassion" as a feeling, as a way of looking with tenderness and understanding at the suffering of others. Compassion is that, but it's also more; it's about action. Compassion is delivering sandwiches to homeless people. Compassion is sending in a donation. Compassion is giving your favorite coat to someone who's shivering. Basically, it's leaving people just a little bit better than the way you found them. I still get teary-eyed sometimes when I remember ways others reached out to me with compassion after my father died. People I hardly knew sent me poems, shared with me memories of my father, and gave me hugs. Compassion needn't be a grand gesture. In fact, it is often the smallest moments of connection that carry us through the tough times.

TRY IT!

Look around you. Who in your life is struggling? Try assisting that person with something you know how to help with. Maybe it's tying shoelaces for a younger sibling. Or tutoring a classmate in spelling or math. Find one simple thing you can do to help, and do it.

COURAGE

Sometimes
courage can be
getting up to face life's
stormy world when you'd rather hide
in bed.

Cinquain: a form that has two syllables in the first line, four in the second line,
six in the third, eight in the fourth, and two in the fifth.

"Maybe Courage is like Memory—a muscle that needs exercise to get strong. So I decided that maybe if I started in a small way, I could gradually work my way up to being brave like the others."

—Geraldine McCaughrean, *The White Darkness*

CHARLES SAYS . . .

There has been many a day, both as a child and as an adult, when I lay in bed, not wanting to get up because of what I'd have to face that day. A test at school, moving day, doing my taxes, traffic, a funeral. However, after waking up, saying the words, "thank you" or "I got this," and making a to-do list of things I need to get done for my day, off I go! After a certain point I realize, to quote the landmark comedy group Monty Python, that I need to "get on with it." It takes courage to face your day, come what may, again and again, with no idea how it will turn out.

TRY IT!

When waking up, try saying the words, "I got this" out loud. It begins your day with a burst of positivity.

CREATE

Gather paint and brush;
lift guitar and strum.
Make something in a mad rush—
who knows what—or who—you'll become?

When you're creating, you can't feel ho-hum;
the voice of your worst critic—you!—will hush
as your imagination begins to thrum.

Soon hope begins to gush,
each new idea a ripe plum.
Feel your face flush—
who knows what—or who—you'll become?

Roundel: an eleven-line poem with three stanzas and
the following rhyme scheme: *abab bab abab*. Line four
repeats as line eleven.

"I'm always thinking about creating. My future starts when I wake up in the morning and see the light."

—Miles Davis

IRENE SAYS . . .

Two things have consistently helped me through tough times: reading books and creating things. It's awfully hard to get bogged down by worry or sadness when you are engaged in the act of creation—and there are so many ways to create! I particularly love creating things out of fabric, like quilts. I enjoy making choices about color, texture, and pattern. I like solving problems and seeing a project come together, even if sometimes that means ripping out seams and starting over. Each quilt tells its own story, and one of the best parts about creating things is sharing them and their stories with others. When you create something, you give the world a piece of yourself and make your corner more beautiful. Making things, creating—it changes you. And often, too, others are changed by your efforts.

TRY IT!

Today, make something new. It could be a song or a poem or a drawing or a scarf or a garden or . . .

Dialogue

We begin   with   love,

but in mere   **nanoseconds**   we plunge into

a furious   **long-distance**   dialogue of

hot words that   **b l a z e**   across the net

like an   **accelerated**   tennis match.

After a marathon   rally,   exhaustion sets in,

good points are made on   **BOTH**   sides

until tempers   **C O O L,**   breathing slows down.

Soon opponents meet   face-to-face,   shake hands, call a truce,

                              end the divide.

Concrete: a poem in which the arrangement of
the type looks like the poem's subject; also called
shaped verse.

"Honesty and openness is always the foundation of insightful dialogue."

—bell hooks

CHARLES SAYS . . .

I've had many disagreements in my life. What I've come away with is sometimes there's validity of both sides of an argument if we cool our jets and try not to be right all the time. There's something to listening, taking in what the other person is saying and letting it settle in. Whether you agree or not is sometimes not the point. The point is listening with an open heart, withholding judgment, and moving on with integrity. To me, that's a common courtesy. I've struggled with in my life, which I'm working hard on rectifying. However, there might be times when it's better to disengage or walk away—when faced with verbal abuse, hate speech, or if you're being provoked. I'm still working on when it's the right time to walk away and when's the right time to stand my ground.

TRY IT!

The next time you're in a disagreement with friends, when you feel a need to chime in with an opinion, try stopping that urge and let them continue. See where it leads you.

DIVERSITY

Diversity is a vibrant patchwork
of colors, civility, opinions
aiming to create one broad tapestry
reflecting this blue-green marble
we each temporarily inhabit.
Let's weave together our differences:
Diversity.

First, let's cut those threads of patriarchy,
its patches have worn out long ago.
Our individual stitches create
this new work of art based on one true thing:
Diversity.

Rondine: a twelve-line poem with seven lines in the first stanza and five lines in the second stanza. Each line is eight or ten syllables except the seventh and twelfth lines. The first word or phrase of the poem becomes a refrain repeated in line seven and twelve.

"'My mama always said piecing quilts is like making friends.' She kept her eyes on the scissors as she cut up a piece of blue ticking. 'Sometimes the more different fabrics—and people— are,' she said, 'the stronger the pattern.'"

—Kirby Larson, *Hattie Big Sky*

CHARLES SAYS . . .

During my college years at Fairleigh Dickinson University in northern New Jersey, I became more fully aware of diversity. I noticed there were wide swaths of fellow students who grew up in economic statuses—both higher and lower—that were far different from mine. I met those who practiced different religions that seemed worlds away than what I had been a part of, and those who didn't have any religious affiliations at all. I also met folks with disabilities, who sometimes struggled navigating around campus, including one whose prosthetic leg once almost disengaged while we were walking outside in between classes. Basically, I saw a microcosm of how the world really is and not the sometimes narrow viewpoint I had while growing up in suburban Philadelphia. The college experience enriched me in ways I still think about to this day. It made me more curious about the world around me, more appreciative of our differences and commonalities and more aware of our shared humanity.

TRY IT!

The next time you go on a class trip, are assigned a group project, or go to a school event, try getting out of your comfort zone and sit with some people who you don't know that well.

DREAM

—found in *Narrative of the Life of Frederick Douglass, an American Slave*, chapter 1

born of cherry-time
a source restless
and quite dark—

a whisper
before sunrise

the light
between hardships
and suffering

tender,
savage wish—

I dare
I expect
I live

Found poem: created by selecting words from an existing text

"SOMETIMES I THINK MY HEAD IS SO BIG BECAUSE IT IS SO FULL OF DREAMS ."

—R. J. Palacio, *Wonder*

IRENE SAYS . . .

I've had all sorts of dreams in my life. When I was in middle school, my dream was to train a horse that my sister would ride to victory in the Kentucky Derby. It didn't make sense because our ponies and horses were pets, not specially trained and pedigreed thoroughbred horses. We had no experience with horse racing. But that didn't stop me; anything is possible. Each day I set about doing what I could to make that dream come true. I read and learned as much as I could about horses. I went to horse camp and helped out at a nearby horse farm. I saved my money, and my sister and I practiced training techniques on our pets. Each step moved me closer to that dream. And then our family moved again—away from horses—and my dream shifted. It's as important to know when to let go of a dream as it is to keep believing in one. Only you can know when that time has come. What's incredible is that there's always another dream waiting in the wings. And sometimes it takes letting go of something to free yourself enough so that you've got strength to grab hold of the next thing.

TRY IT!

Go outside with a loved one at night, when it is quiet and dark and no one is there to poke fun or diminish you. Look at the vast sky, and share your dream out loud—whether it makes sense or not. Offer it to the universe, and come up with one small step you can take toward making that dream a reality—or letting it go.

EMPATHY

Ears open
Mouth closed
Paying
Attention
To the other person
Helping them know
Yes, they matter.

Acrostic: a poem in which the first, last, or other letters in a line create a word or phrase

"Even though I didn't think I'd like empathy it kind of creeps up on you and makes you feel all warm and glowy inside. I don't think I want to go back to life without empathy."

—Kathryn Erskine, *Mockingbird*

CHARLES SAYS . . .

In tenth grade at Penn Wood High School in Lansdowne, Pennsylvania, I was sitting in the lunchroom when my classmates came to me to say that a certain teacher was saying rude things about me behind my back—in particular about how I wasn't as smart as my older brother in the subject she was teaching. I could feel the humiliation wash over me. I went to another teacher named Mrs. Kelly, who I trusted, and voiced my frustration and hurt. Her eyes crinkled in concern as she listened to me vent; her patient listening helped quell some of the pain I was feeling. She even joked with me, which lightened my mood. It took me nearly ten years before I realized even adults make mistakes and are worthy of forgiveness. After all, I have said or done things in my life that I later deduced came from my own frustration, misery, or immaturity. Even though it took me at least a decade to fully forgive this nameless teacher, that healing began with Mrs. Kelly's empathy towards my almost-fifteen-year-old self.

TRY IT!

The next time friends are gossiping about someone else, imagine yourself in that person's shoes, and be the voice to speak up on the other person's behalf.

EQUALITY

slick fashionista
or sweatpants-loving human
we are all equal

whichever features we have,
our bodies don't define us

star student, or one
who doesn't enjoy reading
we are all equal

whichever bathrooms we choose,
each of us wants to feel safe

walk to school each day
or come in a fancy car
we are all equal

whichever language we use,
our words carry equal weight

pray five times a day
or say no prayers at all
we are all equal

whichever land we come from
let's cultivate happiness—

a kind-er world waits
for all of us to catch up
we are all equal

Renga: The first poet writes the first three lines in seventeen syllables. Then the second poet writes two lines containing seven syllables per line.

"When the sun rises, it rises for everyone."
—Cuban proverb

IRENE AND CHARLES SAY . . .

We first began discussing the concept of equality while writing the book *Can I Touch Your Hair? Poems of Race, Mistakes, and Friendship* together. We see equality as the end goal. But equality can't be achieved without *equity*, which refers to treating people fairly, according to their individual needs—something we're learning about every day. We are different people with different needs, but underneath those differences, we are two humans striving for happiness. We are joined by our belief that all people deserve the same opportunity to follow their dreams and experience the world, no matter how different they are from one another.

TRY IT!

Read aloud to someone a book of your choice from the list found on pages 113–115. Have a conversation about what it says to you about equality and equity.

EXERCISE

If you ignore this vessel, if you learn **nothing**
about how to love your body, how **will**
your bones, muscles, organs know to **work**
as one? Your cells will forget themselves **unless**
you move, shake, stretch, sail. Hey, **you:**
celebrate what carries you across currents. It's the least you can **do.**

Golden shovel: inspired by a line of poetry, text, or quote; constructed so that the ending word of each line when read top to bottom composes that line. This poem was built around the quote "Nothing will work unless you do," by Maya Angelou.

> "If you are in a bad mood, go for a walk. If you are still in a bad mood, go for another walk."
>
> —Hippocrates

IRENE SAYS . . .

For years I described myself as "not athletic," until an acquaintance reminded me, "You have a body, don't you? Surely there are some ways you like to move." I sat there silent for a moment—how often have I countered someone's claim of "I'm not creative" with similar words: "You have an imagination, don't you? Surely there's something you like to create." As it turns out, I may not be athletic in the sense of playing a team sport, but I have always enjoyed gentle exercises like walking, stretching, and yoga. And now that I live on a lake, I'm trying things I've never tried before, such as kayaking and paddleboarding. In addition to the more obvious benefits, I also find exercise to be a surefire way out of writer's block—and sometimes even a cure for sadness or depressed feelings.

TRY IT!

Today try a new form of exercise.

EXPERIMENT

The Scientific Method	*for Friendship and* *Self-improvement:*
make observations	*wonder, notice, explore* *yourself and others*
come up with questions	*ask, Can I? Would you? What if?* *knowing each imaginative leap* *may result in flight* *or failure—*
develop hypotheses	*go ahead, consult a crystal ball,* *star chart, history, science,* *and make a prediction* *(the outcome is always uncertain)*
conduct experiments	*just do it!* *a.k.a. trying out an idea* *messing around* *figuring it out*
record results/draw conclusions	*remember: most often,* *you'll be wrong* *any eureka! moments will be short* *and followed by setbacks and* *despair*
share findings	*still: show the world* *what you're learning,* *who you are*

Experimental: exploring and emphasizing innovation (visually, conceptually, or otherwise)

> "Only those of us who carry our cause in our hearts are willing to run the risks."
>
> —Rigoberta Menchú

IRENE SAYS . . .

I was raised in the Episcopal Church, which has a tradition of acolytes. Acolytes are kids, usually between the ages of eight and eighteen, charged with assisting the priests during the service. I thought I would enjoy this role, but at the time, there were no girl acolytes in my church. When I told my father I wanted to be an acolyte, he told me I should approach it like an experiment: gather all the information and then share my findings with the priest. It took some time, but eventually I did become the first girl acolyte in the history of that church. Fortunately, my church was willing to experiment too!

TRY IT!

The next time you are feeling like you don't belong, approach the problem like an experiment. Grab some paper or a poster board, and use the scientific method. Record your observations and make hypotheses. Who knows where you'll end up and what you might achieve!

FORGIVENESS

Forgiveness for what they've done to you.
Forgiveness for feeling guilty too.
Forgive yourself for what you've done.
Please know you're not the only one.

Quatrain: a poem or stanza of four lines. Some are rhymed *aabb* like the one above or *abab* or *abcb*. Other quatrains have no rhymes at all.

"I wondered if that was how forgiveness budded; not with the fanfare of epiphany, but with pain gathering its things, packing up, and slipping away unannounced in the middle of the night."

—Khaled Hosseini, *The Kite Runner*

CHARLES SAYS . . . .

I've said and done some pretty foolish things in my life that I've deeply regretted. It's taken me many years—and I don't still have it licked completely—to forgive myself for some of the things I've said and done when I wasn't my best self *and* to forgive others who have done similar things to me. If I had to choose, though, I'd say forgiving myself is harder. Once I finally do, I can feel the weight of what I carried being lifted off my soul, a clarity takes place, and a new beginning takes hold. I wish the same for you.

TRY IT!

If you feel the need to be forgiven, write a letter of forgiveness to yourself for what you've done and mail it to your own address.

F r e e d o m

Up in the air and over the wall,
I go barefooted.

The leaves, frost-crisp'd break from the trees—
                                    dizzy.

The dark smells sweet, like honey
and full of fire, like ginger.

In my head I hear a humming:
Time to begin!

Cento: composed of lines borrowed from other poems

The lines in this poem originally appeared in the following poems (in order of appearance):
"The Swing" by Robert Louis Stevenson, "Knoxville, Tennessee" by Nikki Giovanni,
"November Night" by Adelaide Crapsey, "I Am Running in a Circle" by Jack Prelutsky, "The
Pony Chair" by Tony Johnston, "Sisters" by Janet S. Wong, "Vacation" by Mary Ann Hoberman,
and "Knock at the Door" by Mother Goose.

"Where freedom is, there shall my country be."

—Latin proverb

IRENE SAYS . . .

One of my most vivid memories of my family's tradition of suppertime discussions centers on this question: "Which is more important to you: money, freedom, love, fame, health, or religion?" My initial response was "love" because isn't that the heart of living? My father might have said "health." My brother, "money." But what we decided was that none of it means anything without FREEDOM. Freedom supersedes all, for what good is love if you are not free to express it? Money is worthless unless you are free to spend it as you like. Fame, health, religion . . . what makes them valuable and precious is the freedom to experience them in your own way. Which is why I am acutely aware of my privilege of being born in a free country—and why my heart aches for those who were not. I honor those (such as refugees fleeing persecution, war, or violence) who are willing to risk all for freedom. And I am so grateful to all those who came before me (like suffragettes!) who paved the way for me to enjoy the freedoms I do have.

TRY IT!

Choose a specific freedom you appreciate. Research current and historical events to better understand, empathize, and acknowledge the people who helped secure this freedom for you. How have you benefited from the work and struggle of others?

FUEL

My journey starts with a full tank on life's uneven road.

Yet never-ending speed bumps and flat tires take me offtrack,
sputtering along, my fuel burning itself to empty.

I pull over to a rest area, eat, nap, replenish my need to succeed
with some *go, go, go* before heading back out. Spirit renewed,
I charge ahead until I find my way back—on track, for now.

Cherita: a three-stanza poem that tells a story. The
first stanza has one line and sets the scene, the second
stanza has two lines, and the third stanza has three lines.

> "No one sees
> the fuel that feeds you."
>
> —Naomi Shihab Nye, excerpt from the poem *"Hidden"*

CHARLES SAYS . . .

Throughout my life, there have been many times when I could feel my personal gas tank running on empty. For example, schoolwork, class bullies, and sports have now changed into author visits, deadlines, and paying bills. When my tank gets empty and I need to refuel, a nap is often just what I need. Think of naps as a recharging of your spirit, so when it's time to face life's new obstacles, you'll be ready to go, go, go. I also recharge by reading poems and letters written by students that teachers have shared with me after visiting their schools. When I look at them, I feel like Irene and I are making a difference, that we're being heard, and that the students are being heard as well.

TRY IT!

What's your way of refueling when *you're* all tapped out? Hanging out with friends, reading a book, exercising, or playing video games? Whatever it may be, carve out some time to do it at least once a week.

GRATITUDE

When lightning splits the oak,
it is you, Gratitude, who helps us
appreciate the years
Oak shaded our summers.

When the answer is no
instead of yes—O Gratitude!
it is you who says,
this is how we learn.

When our carefully laid plans
fail to bear fruit,
it is you, Gentle Teacher, who shows us
there are many ways

to live a life.

Ode: a poem of praise

> "Turn your face toward the sun and
> the shadows fall behind you."
>
> —Maori proverb

IRENE SAYS . . .

One summer my parents left me for two weeks at my grandparents' house in
Port St. Joe, Florida. I adored my grandparents, but two weeks is a long time!
I got really homesick. What helped me through it was Grandma Dykes' corn
bread and daily trips to the library. These two things were the beginnings of a
"gratitude list," though I didn't know to call it that at the time. These days, instead
of wallowing whenever I feel sorry for myself, I make a gratitude list right away.
Just a simple list of all the things I am grateful for right now, this moment. It helps
me remember that I am not alone and that things aren't as bad as they seem.

TRY IT!

Make a gratitude list of your own.

(EPITAPH FOR)

HATE

Here lies
fear of what's different,
quiet oppression,
invisible walls
and microaggression.

Forever gone
police brutality,
discrimination,
snap judgments
based on misinformation.

Here lies hate,
May unity swallow the grave.

Epitaph: written upon death; words engraved
on a tombstone

"Fear of something is at the root of hate for others, and hate within will eventually destroy the hater."

—George Washington Carver

IRENE SAYS . . .

In my family, we were not allowed to use the word *hate*, even though there were times when I "hated" my brothers or "hated" peas or "hated" the fact that we were moving yet again. My mom taught me that underneath the word *hate*, there is almost always another emotion: fear, anger, sadness, or frustration. I wonder sometimes how different the world would be if we all turned over that rock of hate and looked underneath with curiosity—what's really going on? How would it change the ways in which we relate to one another?

TRY IT!

The next time you hear yourself—or someone else— say the word *hate*, turn over the metaphorical rock and see what emotion lurks underneath.

HOPE

Fierce
camel
carries us
across deserts
without faltering,
thick eyelashes batting
sand, hooves steadily clopping
toward oasis shimmering
its promise: *All travelers welcome!*

Nonet: a nine-line poem that begins with a one-syllable line and builds to a nine-syllable line, or the reverse

"No matter how much sadness there is in life, there are equal amounts of maybe-things'll-get-better-someday-soon."

—Pam Muñoz Ryan, *Echo*

IRENE SAYS . . .

Hope often comes from unexpected sources. Once, when our family had just moved (for the ninth time!), my parents got me a white fluffball of an American spitz puppy. Her name was Sasha. It was Sasha who helped carry me across the desert of adjusting to a new home and missing my old home. She played with me and listened to me and was tolerant of my attempts at grooming and training. No matter how tough my day at school, Sasha was there waiting for me all bright eyes and wagging tail whenever I stepped off the bus.

TRY IT!

What can you do right now to help carry someone across a desert? To make "all travelers welcome?" Try positivity: acknowledging someone's efforts, expressing optimism for the future. Offer an encouraging word to someone today.

Humility doesn't seek praise
in a world busy shouting, *look at me!*
It says, *I'm sorry*, and learns from mistakes.
Humility doesn't seek praise
or use a perfection stick to measure the days.
It says, *I don't know*, and, *help me, please?*
Humility doesn't seek praise
in a world busy shouting, *look at me!*

Triolet: a poem with eight lines in which line one repeats in lines four and seven and line two repeats in line eight to create the following rhyme scheme: *abaaabab*

> "I've always admired a person who can admit to not knowing something. Most people smile and nod and pretend they know everything for fear of being caught out. But those people only ensure their ignorance."
>
> —Jonathan Auxier, *Sweep: The Story of a Girl and Her Monster*

IRENE SAYS . . .

When I was in middle school I tried to hide my imperfections with clothes, makeup, and by keeping quiet when I wasn't sure of the answer to a question. That's because I thought people would like me better if I appeared more perfect than I actually am. It turns out the opposite is true: by sharing my imperfections, admitting when I am wrong, I open myself to connecting with others over our shared humanness. These days I have an opportunity each day to practice this kind of humility as I continue a new hobby: playing the cello. It's not an easy instrument to learn at any age. But if you want to get better—a anything—you have to be willing to fail, to make mistakes. And perhaps the simplest act of humility is admitting one's imperfections, saying "I don't know and asking for help.

TRY IT!

Today do something new and allow yourself to make a mistake. Ask yourself: Wh am I learning? Share the experience with another person.

INTENTION

My mind is sometimes like a charcoal-infused
silvery cloud weighed down by this
complicated planet around me.

When life overwhelms my spirit, rather
than lashing out, creating a downpour
of fury due to stormy temper tantrums,
I instead take a deep breath, adjust my thinking
then decide to be gentle, like a drizzle, nurturir.
our habitat instead of trying to destroy it.

Each time I give myself a personal
intervention to shift my thoughts
with a positive, clear intention—
sunshine cascades into my world.

Didactic: an instructional poem that dispenses a clear messa

"I believe the choice to be excellent begins with aligning your thoughts and words with the intention to require more from yourself."

—Oprah Winfrey

CHARLES SAYS . . .

When I was first getting into children's poetry, I would go to the 8-1-1 section of the library, see the spines of poetry books lined up with the authors' last names, and think, "I have stories to tell too. Wouldn't it be nice if one day there were books that had my name on them?" And so it's happened. It didn't start off that way. I had my poems and manuscripts rejected for years, working jobs I didn't like while I pursued this passion of mine. Did I get frustrated? Yes. Did I get furious with the way my life was going? Sometimes. However, things didn't start getting better until I shifted my outlook by focusing on the positive and not the negative. I was pursuing something I loved, with the intention to one day make a living writing and performing my own poems. When you have clear intentions, from a pure place in your heart, nothing or no thing can stop you.

TRY IT!

What is something you felt compelled to do because your heart tells you to, rather than something you've been *told* to do? Whatever it is, please consider writing it down, and pursuing it.

JUSTICE

Innocent blood spilling down our street.
When are we gonna get justice?

Poisoned water in what we drink and eat.
When are we gonna get justice?

Abusers in positions of power.
When are we gonna get justice?

Time to come down from your ivory tower.
When are we gonna get justice?

Repeat offenders who get off scot-free.
When are we gonna get justice?

This is not how our world's supposed to be.
When are we gonna get justice?

World, make way for this wall of resisters.
When are we going to get justice?

Let's stay united, brothers and sisters.
When are we gonna get justice?

Our march for equality's far from done.
When are we gonna get justice?

We won't stop till we're united as one.
We won't stop till we ALL get justice!

Chant: a short, simple melody, especially one characterized
by repetition used in group settings

"Where justice is denied, where poverty is enforced, where ignorance prevails, and where any one class is made to feel that society is an organized conspiracy to oppress, rob, and degrade them, neither persons nor property will be safe."

—Frederick Douglass

CHARLES SAYS . . .

My great-grandmother, Marguerite Stocker, worked as a house cleaner in Philadelphia, Pennsylvania. She had to clean three houses a day. The houses weren't close to one another either, so she had to take a trolley car to get to each place. One time, while heavily pregnant, after working all day, she got on a trolley car where all the seats were filled with white people. Not one of them offered their seat to her.

As my great-grandparents on both sides of my family continued working in jobs where subtle and not-so-subtle racism was the course of the day, they kept believing in justice. They sacrificed for a better life for their children, which got passed to their grandchildren, then to my generation and, now, to my nieces, nephews, cousins, and beyond. We're all navigating an easier path because of them.

TRY IT!

Ask members of your family (parents, grandparents, aunts, uncles, cousins) about your family history and what positive and, perhaps, not-so-positive roles your ancestors played in the world they lived in, specifically regarding their roles in the justices and injustices of that time period. What can you learn from their stories?

KINDNESS

Kindness boards a bus.

Kindness stands
so you can sit.

Kindness unwraps
a sandwich
and gives you the bigger half.

Cherita: a three-stanza poem that tells a story. The first stanza has one line and sets the scene, the second stanza has two lines, and the third stanza has three lines.

"But remember, boy, that a kind act can sometimes be as powerful as a sword."

—Rick Riordan, *The Battle of the Labyrinth*

IRENE SAYS . . .

Each evening when I think back over my day, it is often the small kindnesses and simple courtesies that stand out: an unexpected smile, a letter from a friend, the stranger in a store who returned the button that fell from my blouse. Being kind and using good manners cost nothing, yet they create so much goodwill. And I find that when I am kind, when I reach out to others in small ways, it makes ME feel better too.

TRY IT!

Start a "Catch 'Em Being Kind" campaign. Ask your teacher to donate some bulletin board space, and in one corner add an envelope of paper slips. Whenever you witness someone else's act of kindness, write it on a slip and pin it to the board. Invite others to do the same, and soon that bulletin board will be covered in kind deeds.

LAUGHTER

Laughter is a hippopotamus
who has a new place to sleep.
It's so grateful for these surroundings
that it commences to . . . *weep*.

It sobs on the floor, howls on the roof,
blubbers on tables and chairs,
whimpers against each of our walls,
then wails on all of the stairs.

Our house is a heap of destruction.
My family's *so* upset.
Why don't they all look on the bright side?
Laughter's like a brand-new pet!

Nonsense: a form of light verse, usually for children, depicting imaginative characters in amusing situations of fantasy. It is whimsical in tone and with a rhythmic appeal, often employing fanciful phrases and meaningless made-up words.

> "There is nothing more precious than laughter."
> —Frida Kahlo, *The Diary of Frida Kahlo: An Intimate Self-Portrait*

CHARLES SAYS . . .

I have had moments when, at least a few times a week, a piece of light verse poetry has brought a smile to my face and provided me with some much-needed laughter. It has given me a respite from whatever was bothering me at the time. I first got into nonsense verse by performing the poems of Jack Prelutsky, Judith Viorst, and others before delving into the work of poets Dorothy Parker, J. Patrick Lewis, and more.

TRY IT!

Go to your library, at school or in your community. Ask the librarian for a book of light verse from section 8-1-1, read one poem aloud, and see how you feel. I have a strong suspicion laughter may ensue. Afterward, consider checking the book out of the library

LISTEN

Foggy thoughts
open up
to clear sky.

As my friend
leans forward,
gently nods,

eyes zeroed
straight on me—
listening.

Tricubes: three stanzas, three lines, and three
syllables per line. That's it!

"Even the silence has a story to tell you. Just listen. Listen."

—Jacqueline Woodson, *Brown Girl Dreaming*

CHARLES SAYS . . .

Like the friendship of the characters in our first book together, my friendship with Irene has deepened over time. I've shared my thoughts and worries about a myriad of things in my life, some of which I've never shared with anyone else. Irene listens without judgment, hoping the best for me and giving advice when I ask for her opinion. She's a world champion listener. Afterward, I feel better, understood, and valued. To listen is to respect, to let a person know they matter. I'm grateful to my poetic forever friend for listening to me.

TRY IT!

Pay attention to how much you talk when in a conversation. Keep a tally: How many times are you interrupting? Are you hearing everything or most of the things the other person is telling you? You can find out by repeating to the other person what you think you just heard them say—and waiting for them to tell you if you are correct.

LOVE

Love in the time of racism
requires
cardinal's
red
courage,
requires
bluebird
carrying
sky,
requires
love—no time for racism.

Skinny: an eleven-line poem in which the first and eleventh
lines use all or mostly the same words and the second, sixth,
and tenth lines are identical. Shorter lines are preferred for
the first and eleventh lines. All other lines are one word

> "If you have no intention of loving or being loved, then the whole journey is pointless."
>
> —Kate DiCamillo, *The Miraculous Journey of Edward Tulane*

IRENE SAYS . . .

When I count my blessings, chief among them is the good fortune to have been born into a family where I was well-loved. It's one of many privileges I've enjoyed, and I know all humans deserve the same love. I'm also privileged in other ways, because I was born white. This fact was driven home to me a few years ago when I was conversing with the mother of one of my son's best friends. We were discussing whether to allow the kids to walk five blocks from their school to a restaurant in downtown Birmingham, Alabama. When the other mother expressed some concerns about safety, I agreed, remembering the large group of homeless people who liked to hang out on one of the corners. The other mother said, "It's not the homeless people I'm worried about. It's the police." Because her son has dark skin, she was concerned that he might become a news story like Trayvon Martin or Tamir Rice, something that had never occurred to me because my child's skin is white. I would like to live in a world where everyone is loved—homeless people and police too—and no mother has to worry about the safety of her child walking down the street.

TRY IT!

Write a poem about something you love that a lot of other people don't: a certain musical group, stormy weather, brussels sprouts. What courage does it take to love this thing? What unique qualities are most endearing to you? Be as specific as possible.

MINDFULNESS

one single moment
an ocean broken open—
thoughts jellyfish
along accepting currents,
you drift buoyant

Tanka: a five-line poem in the Japanese haiku tradition that can be written with a five/seven/five/seven/seven syllable count or by the following line pattern: short, long, short, long, long. The third line is a pivot line.

> If you can't live longer, live deeper.
>
> —Italian proverb

IRENE SAYS . . .

A poet's job is to "explode" the moment. That means we take something small and make it big in a poem. We pay attention with all of our senses. We allow thoughts and feelings to come and go. So, really, to write a poem is to be in a state of mindfulness. And I like to think the reverse is also true: to be in a state of mindfulness is to live a poem. It's how my blog got its name: *Live Your Poem*. It's something to strive for, isn't it? To explode each moment, to pay attention with all our senses, to be engaged with the art of living each and every moment. Imagine if we all went through our days with this kind of focus—no doubt the world would become a more beautiful place just by our attention to it.

TRY IT!

Choose one small thing—the moment when you are brushing your teeth or when you take that first gulp of your favorite drink—and be fully there. Explode the moment. What do you see, taste, hear, smell, feel? See how this kind of close attention changes you and your world.

NATURE

rain taps face
as black-capped chickadee sings—
morning baptism

Haiku: a Japanese form traditionally evoking images of the natural world. Some have seventeen syllables in three lines of five/seven/five, although that's not a mandatory rule.

"The best remedy for those who are afraid, lonely, or unhappy is to go outside, somewhere where they can be quite alone with the heavens, nature, and God. Because only then does one feel that all is as it should be and that God wishes to see people happy, amidst the simple beauty of nature. As long as this exists, and it certainly always will, I know that then there will always be comfort for every sorrow, whatever the circumstances may be. And I firmly believe that nature brings solace in all troubles."

—Anne Frank, *The Diary of a Young Girl*

CHARLES SAYS . . .

Walking in nature is a balm to my soul. I appreciate the universe more when I see what wonders Mother Nature has created. Also, I love, love, *love* walking in drizzle. Hearing the rhythmic beats of rain, even having some splash on my face despite my umbrella, is a big stress reliever. I especially enjoy hearing the sounds of birds still chirping in the trees, determined to stay put. They're troopers. Fresh air, occasional drizzle, chirping birds . . . *ahhhh.*

TRY IT!

Go to a park. Take a walk or ride a bike.

NETIQUETTE

What if you're feeling forgotten
and start fishing for *likes*?

What if it's a boring morning
and you type something
that creates a maelstrom?

What if you never check
the bias of others—
or your own?

What if you send a picture
and that picture ends up
on the phones of all the people you know—
and even more you *don't* know?

What if you forget your audience
may include your teachers,
                    your parents,
the very person you are talking about?

What if instead of responding in anger,
you wait ten minutes,
            an hour,
                a day?

What if you decide
to treat each keystroke
as if your life—
or someone else's life—
depends upon it?

| Question poem: | a poem composed entirely of questions | |

"Be civil to all; sociable to many; familiar with few; friend to one; enemy to none."

—Benjamin Franklin

IRENE SAYS . . .

While I love how social media allows us to connect with others more easily than ever before, it's also a source of anxiety for me. There are so many ways to mess up! When we're looking at a computer screen instead of into someone's eyes, we can forget how harmful and hurtful words can be. Sometimes these platforms that are intended to provide a virtual bridge actually end up making me feel isolated and alone. I've experienced firsthand the punch of someone's comment, and more than one person dear to me has resorted to self-harm as a result of an online interaction gone bad. I know with certainty that I have typed and sent messages via social media that have caused pain, and I wish I could take them all back! It's impossible to know how people will receive our words online. But there are safeguards we can take, such as the ones mentioned in this poem. Just like during in-person interactions, simple courtesies can make all the difference.

TRY IT!

Look back over this poem, and choose one question to apply to your online life right now, today.

OPEN

Despite this
fury of hatred
that tries to
extinguish
equal opportunity,
our hearts stay open.

hadorma: a form consisting of a six-line stanza. The syllable count
three/five/three/three/seven/five. You can also have an unlimited
mber of three lines or multiple stanzas in a poem.

"Let us catch ourselves opening
and then catch ourselves stopping

and not. Let us open and open,
without knowing how."

—Billy Merrell, excerpt from the poem "Moth"

CHARLES SAYS . . .

Being open to change, being open to a better world, is hard because of the resistance you may find. There's also a fair share of irony if you used to be one of the resisters. For example, I used to look at vegans as if they were from another planet. How dare they talk about animal rights, refusing to consume dairy, eat meat, or wear clothing or shoes made from animals? "What weird people," I thought. I'd also say to myself, "I'm a grown man. I'll do what I want, when I want, how I want. I'm not going to listen to anyone talk to me about veganism!" However, I finally saw the reasons why it made sense, as well as how much better eating plant-based foods made me feel once I tried it. After that happened, I knew I was saying goodbye to a previous way of life because, eventually, my heart was open to it. While I did, and still do, get a negative comment every now and then, I've found most people to be respectful. Becoming a vegan was one of the smarter decisions I've made as an adult.

TRY IT!

When you hear about something new to you, instead of immediately dismissing it, try investigating it instead. Watch videos or read about it. Then make up your mind. However, it's important to find reputable sources, because there are plenty of ideas on the internet that are flat-out wrong or even dangerous.

PAUSE

My family may have its flaws
but once we're together we pause
to give thanks and grace
before it's a race
to stuff food into our jaws.

Limerick: a humorous rhyming verse of three long lines, then two short lines. The rhyme scheme is *aabba*.

"We will be more successful in all our endeavors if we can let go of the habit of running all the time, and take little pauses to relax and re-center ourselves. And we'll also have a lot more joy in living."

—Thich Nhat Hanh

CHARLES SAYS . . .

I'm mighty amused every time members of the Waters family have a meal together. All you can usually hear are forks, spoons, and knives clanking against the plates and bowls. Hardly a word is said because we're not there to chatter; we're there to partake in the grub lovingly assembled for our nourishment. After a while, people do in fact start talking again, especially when the older generation, of which I'm now a member, shares funny childhood stories. (Like the time when I used to be a pancake-eating machine!) In our busy lives, it's important to slow down and spend some time with family, savoring the time we have with older and younger generations.

TRY IT!

Before sitting down to eat, go around the table and take a moment to say what you are thankful for.

PEACE

If only it came
foil-wrapped
with a creamy
center—

I'd take a bite
and you'd take a bite

and for an instant
all our struggles
and opinions,

our this-is-me-this-is-you
battle lines

would turn dark,
bittersweet,
milky

and then even that
would disappear,

leaving our mouths
soft

and thick
with hope.

Free verse: verse that does not follow a fixed metrical pattern

> "If you cannot find peace within yourself, you will never find it anywhere else."
>
> —Marvin Gaye

IRENE SAYS . .

I'm a middle child, and middle children are often known as "peacemakers." We want everyone to be happy! My name, "Irene," even means "peace." I've always loved that, and I do think it's shaped me in many ways. A friend once nicknamed me serene Irene, and I had to laugh because often I can appear serene on the outside when my thoughts and feelings are churning on the inside! Truly, peace is a practice. And we get better at it the more we practice both stillness of body and stillness of mind. One thing I like to do is meditate. There are all kinds of apps and online sources for this. Other forms of meditation for me include writing poetry and indulging in my daily dark chocolate habit. That's right: chocolate! Something about that creamy, delicious comfort fills me with a sense of calm and rightness, and then I am able to bring more peace to the world around me.

TRY IT!

Think of a way you can create peace in your own life—maybe it's meditation or chocolate or something else. Make it a daily practice, and see how it changes your world.

QUESTION

Ask a question when you don't know what to do;
ask a question when you're wondering *why*.
Questions are the way to learn anything new.
Want to know what is real? Here's a clue—
Pry, spy! (Remember: Respectfulness rules apply.)
Ask a question! When you don't know what to do

you can't assume everything you read or hear is true.
It pays to identify, simplify, and verify.
Questions are the way to learn anything new.

Exploring all sides of a story can be a virtue.
Sometimes the hero turns out to be a bad guy.
Ask a question when you don't know. What to do?

Read, Google, interview.
Everyone can be a private eye—
Questions are the way to learn anything new.

The answers wait patiently for you—
go forth! Don't allow ignorance to multiply.
Ask a question when you don't know what to do.
Questions are the way to learn anything new.

Villanelle: a nineteen-line poem with two
rhymes throughout, consisting of five
tercets and a quatrain, with the first and
third lines of the opening tercet recurring
alternately at the end of the other tercets
and with both repeated at the close of the
concluding quatrain

"How are you going to find out about things if you don't ask questions?"

—L. M. Montgomery, *Anne of Green Gables*

IRENE SAYS . . .

I met Cindy, my best friend in college, during my first social work class. She was funny, smart, caring, and we became instant friends. Cindy is blind, and she used a white walking stick to get around campus. Often she would grab my arm and allow me to guide her. From the first day I met Cindy, I wanted to know everything about her experience with blindness, but it seemed rude to ask. Was she blind from birth? Did she want a guide dog? Eventually she saved me by saying, "All you have to do is ask permission to ask the questions." She said that she'd been waiting for my questions about her blindness and that it was equally as maddening when a person didn't ask—essentially ignoring the ways she was different—as when they treated her like an exhibit at the zoo by asking inappropriate questions. Cindy's the one who taught me that one way to be respectfully curious is to first ask for consent. After I realized I didn't have to avoid talking with her about her blindness, our friendship really deepened.

TRY IT!

The next time you're curious about a person's experiences, start by asking them if it's okay for you to ask a few questions. Allow their comfort level to guide the conversation from there.

REACH

after creation of Adam
by Michelangelo

To live in that moment
before touch,

in the breath
between fingers,

where what comes before—
or after—
ceases to matter.

To risk rebuke, rebuff, rejection.

To risk falling,
failing.

To fall—

all for the possibility
of rising
together.

Ekphrasis: inspired by a piece of art

> ## "I decided I wasn't going to come down. I was going to fly. I was going to stay up in the air forever."
>
> —Jesse Owens, *on his final leap in the 1935 Big Ten Championships long-jump competition, a record-breaking 26.67 feet (8.13 m), a record that remained unbroken for twenty-five years*

IRENE SAYS . . .

Sometimes the hardest thing for me is reaching out to another person. I'm shy and introverted, and I am completely okay with my own company. And inviting others into my world is a lot of work. It's also a risk: I don't want to be rebuffed or rejected. It still feels like a miracle to me whenever I reach and the other person reaches back. That's what it was like when Charles said yes to my invitation to write poems together. I never could have imagined we'd not only write that book together but this one as well—and enjoy an abiding friendship through it all! That kind of thing can never happen if you don't first reach . . . which is why the only way to really fail is to stop trying.

TRY IT!

Sometimes you have to "fake it till you make it." So today assume a confident mind-set, even if it doesn't come naturally to you. Force yourself past your fears of rejection by focusing on the wonderful possibilities that can unfold when you invite someone new into your life. Be the one to reach out first.

RELEAS E

Our time together . . . extinguished.
Its flame, an apparition.
At last, I release you with love.

Goodbye.

Naani: consists of four lines totaling twenty to twenty-five
syllables. It's not bound by any particular subject.

> "If you don't release the something, it just weighs you down until you can hardly move."
>
> —Erin Entrada Kelly, *Hello, Universe*

CHARLES SAYS . . .

There have been times—both long ago and not so long ago—when friendships have ended, and I wondered what happened. Specifically, I was focused on who was wrong and who was right. In the end, I think, for the most part, both parties do things that cause a friendship to end . . . so, for the sake of my well-being, I've done my best to move on, not in an angry way, but with love, wishing the other person the best, as we both continue on life's journey. I'm not going to lie—I didn't always feel this way. It took time as I've matured as an adult. I hope you mature faster than I did! Ultimately, picking up the pieces and getting on with your life is one of the best ways of not only loving yourself but making the world better.

TRY IT!

Write the name of a person who hurt you on a stone. Chant this poem as you toss the stone into a body of water.

RESPECT

Dear Ms. Franklin,

You strong, proud, unapologetic goddess of music.
<u>Ain't No Way</u> I could ever consider this world without
your three-octave-and-rising vocal pyrotechnics of soul.
<u>I Say a Little Prayer</u> that your spirit is released,
at peace from cancer's unsentimental clutches.

From a gospel-singing child at your father's church
to making our 44th US president weep from
the awe of you being such <u>A Natural Woman</u>,
goodness knows the pain and joy you've seen as this
country attempts to figure out what it is.

Yet you remained <u>Rock Steady</u> asking us to <u>Think</u>
about consequences for our actions for any <u>Chain of fools</u>
who try to stamp out this American Dream we have of
living in peace. I found out what life really means
to me by thinking of you with (R-E-S-P-E-C-T.)

    Rest Easy, <u>Angel</u>
    LUV,
    Your biggest fan

Epistle: a letter poem that takes the idea of formal letters and applies poetic devices to them. The one general rule is the letter has to be addressed to someone or something. Epistles can be used in different poetic writing forms.

> ### "She needed a hero, so that's what she became."
>
> —Jane from the TV series *Jane the Virgin*

CHARLES SAYS . . . .

The older I've gotten, the more I see how much privilege I've had as a boy and now as a man, and how many glass ceilings have yet to be broken by the girls and women in our world. From wage equality to holding more seats in political offices and boardrooms to being treated with respect. I used to dismiss some women's voices out of my own ego and stubbornness. I don't anymore. I'm sorry I did in the first place.

This makes me grateful to have women in my life who have helped me along the way to become a better person through their kindness and strength. As a man, I continue to ask questions, make mistakes, and learn from the strong women who've enriched my life . . . the sheroes.

TRY IT!

Who are the sheroes in your life? Find them and thank them for being beacons of light in this sometimes dark, perplexing cosmos we occupy. Also, ask them for advice about how you can follow in their footsteps.

TEAM

In spite of resistance from ourselves due
to pockets of infighting, vile words,
opposing teams, we link arms in
kinship, stitched together by
this life force called "change." We
kick off our journey
as family.
Our unit
stands as
one.

Etheree: a ten-line poem that begins with ten-syllables
and works its way to one-syllable or the reverse

"Abi yu ngir.
Unity is strength."

—Common phrase in Limbum, a language spoken by
the Wimbum people, primarily in Cameroon

CHARLES SAYS . . .

When I was part of the football team, wrestling squad, and baseball team as a teenager, I had teammates with their own agendas who didn't care about the team. I also had teammates who were supportive, not only of myself, but also of other members of the squad. I had coaches who cared about me and my progression as an athlete and person, coaches who were cruel, and coaches who were sometimes both, which really threw me for a loop. Figuring out how to navigate those choppy currents as a young person helped me when I became an adult. All you have to do is replace the word *teammate* with *coworker*, and the word *coach* with *boss*. Somehow, with all the drama that swirled around our teams, when it was time to play, we put aside all that nonsense and got the job done together. I'm thankful for both the good and not-so-good times in organized sports because they made me a stronger individual, and perhaps, more importantly, they helped me become more selfless.

TRY IT!

Join a team—at your place of worship, at your school, or in your community. If there isn't a team for the thing you're passionate about, be the one to start it. Set a date, put up some flyers, and make it happen!

TENACITY

Tenacity is bursting with determination,
tunneling under enemy lines
like a gopher, stuffing positive words—
belief, strength, willpower—
into its large cheek pouches,
refusing to allow other words—
can't, no, quit—
to blight its soul.
Tenacity excavates hard lessons
along its path:
traps, dead ends, floods.
Tenacity will never stop trudging
across Earth's deep, ragged, rich soil.

Free verse: verse that does not follow a
fixed metrical pattern

> "Let me tell you the secret that has led me to my goal. My strength lies solely in my tenacity."
>
> —Louis Pasteur

CHARLES SAYS . . .

As a professional actor, I've appeared in regional, summer stock, and dinner theaters, as well as theatrical tours, theme parks, commercials, television shows, and movies. To get those opportunities, I've auditioned for many, many hundreds of people and been rejected many, many hundreds of times. I've also worked more than a few survival jobs to keep financially afloat—including security guard, warehouse worker, market researcher, restaurant server, shuttle driver, and more. What got me through it all was a belief in myself and the courage to keep going. To have the tenacity to not give up on my goals, to persevere knowing good things would happen to me eventually if I hung in there.

TRY IT!

Create a vision board with a list of goals you have, and put the board on your wall so you can look at them daily.

UPSTANDER

Upstander, you
have words
I want:
No,
Stop!

You say,
Welcome,
you can sit
by me.

Your actions
show me
different
is magnificent.

Upstander,
you give me
courage
to be
an upstander too.

Apostrophe: a form in which the
speaker directly addresses a
person, place, thing, or idea

"If you have the feeling that something is wrong, don't be afraid to **SPEAK UP**."

—Fred Korematsu

IRENE SAYS . . .

Speaking up on someone else's behalf can be difficult. While I am eager to comfort and encourage a victim, it's difficult for me to tell the aggressor to stop, or to call for help. And I know it's not just me: I remember a reality show where an altercation was staged in a public park, just to see if anyone would intervene. Most people walked the other way or shouted at the victim to get away. Finally, someone was brave enough to address the perpetrator. It helps us all to see others step up, either in real life or in books and movies. I'm a huge fan of the Harry Potter series, and I love how Harry repeatedly acts as an upstander to bullies like Draco Malfoy and Severus Snape on behalf of people like Neville Longbottom. Harry Potter is a hero in so many ways!

TRY IT!

Think of your favorite book, comic, or real-life superhero. In what way is that superhero also an upstander? The next time you are faced with a situation, ask yourself "What would my superhero do?" and act accordingly.

VOICE

I like to shout
loud, proud,
strong words

I like to whisper
tender,
remember-me words

Words have Power

words can split a city
with the speed
of an earthquake

words can rain down,
bringing spring bouquets
to a barren desert

Words have Power

like a supermoon,
words can illuminate
the darkest hollows

like a river,
words can smooth
stones of hurt

Words have Power

Please tell me
your feelings
and opinions

Please speak to me
with love
and honesty

Words have Power

what's the point
of having a voice?

what's the reason
for all these words?

Words make the world better

sharing our words

listening to each
other

can bring us together

today

and tomorrow

Words have Power!

Poem in two voices: written in two columns where two
different characters converse about a subject

"I have come to believe over and over again that what is most important to me must be spoken, made verbal and shared, even at the risk of having it bruised or misunderstood."

—Audre Lorde

IRENE AND CHARLES SAY . . .

We live in a noisy world. With so many voices clamoring for our attention via the internet, social media, TV, billboards, and more, it can be difficult to hear our own voices, much less the voices of others. This was made clear to us when we were sharing *Can I Touch Your Hair?* at East Grand Rapids Middle School in Michigan. We were talking with the Diversity Group—students particularly interested in promoting diversity and inclusiveness at their school. It was only after we stopped talking and opened the floor to their questions that magic—and change!—began to happen. We learned that morning how vital it is to use good manners and to have a *discussion*, not just a presentation.

TRY IT!

How will you use your voice? Maybe it's creating a podcast, writing a poem, giving a speech, or creating a protest sign. Share your voice—in your way—with the world today.

VULNERABLE

Brave front disintegrates when I see Mom,
post-seizure in hospital gown, vulnerable.
My clenched throat sputters out, "I'm scared." Mom says,
"I'm okay." When her ashen hand reaches for mine—
I feel my heart dissolve.

Gogyoshi: a five-line poem. There are no other rules.

"When we were children, we used to think that when we were grown-up we would no longer be vulnerable. But to grow up is to accept vulnerability . . . To be alive is to be vulnerable."

—Madeleine L'Engle, *Walking on Water: Reflections on Faith and Art*

CHARLES SAYS . . .

As a kid, I used to try to be macho, imitating what I saw guys doing at school and on television. A lot of that changed, the day before my thirteenth birthday. Early that Sunday morning, my mother had a nocturnal seizure. Help arrived before she died or suffered irreparable damage, but in the blink of an eye, my family could have changed forever. As she was being carried out by the paramedics, I acted like it wasn't a big deal. But when I visited her in the hospital the next day, any machismo I felt disappeared—I was terrified. Thankfully, Mom recovered. After that incident, I did my best to be more attentive—accomplishing my daily chores without being reminded, thanking her more often after meals, keeping my mouth shut when helping put together the twenty-three bags of laundry for our weekly family trip to the laundromat. Even though I didn't realize it at the time, Mom's unfortunate episode was the beginning of a new way of life for me. Every conversation could be the last one. I learned to show my true feelings more often, even if someone said I was too "soft," or that I needed to "be a man."

TRY IT!

Write about a time in your life when something bad happened unexpectedly. How vulnerable did you feel when you let your guard down?

(BEAR) WITNESS

Tell the stories that name your pain—
bring your suffering into light.
With the faith of a lost kite,
dive headlong into biting rain.
Let your words howl and hurricane.
When you speak weak and bleary-eyed,
when you scream though you'd rather hide,
your stories wing into warm air;
your suffering becomes prayer.
Healing waits on the other side.

Decima: a ten-line poem popular in Puerto Rico with eight
syllables per line in the following rhyme pattern: *abbaaccddc*

"For the dead and the living, we must bear witness."

—Elie Wiesel

IRENE SAYS . . .

To bear witness means to share our stories. It's a time to let down our guard and be our true selves. It's a way of saying, "this is me" and "you're not alone" and "we matter." It's been my honor and privilege to bear witness with others throughout my life, both as a speaker and a listener. Healing happens when the story is no longer trapped within a person, when the truth of a person's experience has been acknowledged. One meaningful way to bear witness is to read books about people's pain or books that recount tragedies in history. I think it's why I've always been drawn to historical fiction and memoirs. By reading books like *Anne Frank: The Diary of a Young Girl* and *The Red Badge of Courage*, I learned that writing can also be a powerful way to bear witness. These kinds of books made me want to be a writer—so that I too might bear witness and connect with others through my experiences and imagination.

TRY IT!

Today bear witness by reading a book about a true-life event. Or visit a memorial or museum, and share your experience by writing about it.

W NDER

I sit on my bed, staring out at apartment complexes
across a sea of grass as skeletal branches shiver
against the cold snap enveloping our neighborhood.
I'm curious about many things, I possess such an array
of questions dealing with this life of mine, I can
barely keep up with the speed of my own thoughts.

These are some of the things I wonder about.

Why am I burdened with this constant need to talk?
Consistently testing the patience of even the kindest
of humans? I wonder when I grow up am I going to
be a firefighter, helping to extinguish blazes while
saving lives? Or become a stutter-step, spinning,
slam-dunking basketball player in the NBA?
Or will I still be an unpopular, dragon-breath-
smelling, yellow-teeth-having pip-squeak?

These are some of the things I wonder about.

I could, at least, attempt to reduce my constant jabbering,
become better friends with a toothbrush, toothpaste,
mouthwash, and floss. I realize, to quote Grandpa,
"In the end, everything will be all right." However,
I'm still curious about the person I will morph into;
if life will be kind to me. I hope so.

These are some of the things I wonder about.

The Bop: a form with three stanzas. There is a refrain after each stanza. The first stanza
consists of a problem being presented in six lines. The second stanza expands the problem
through exploration in eight lines. The third stanza either shows the failed attempt to resolve
the problem or presents a solution in six lines.

> # "Wonder is the feeling of a philosopher, and philosophy begins in wonder."
>
> —Socrates , in Plato's *Theaetetus*

CHARLES SAYS . . .

When I was a child, I would stand next to my bedroom window, staring out into the world and wondering what my life would be like when I grew up. The older I've gotten, the more my sense of wonder has expanded: I'm now fascinated by everything from how leaves change their color to how we're all made of star stuff and live our lives on a planet spinning through space. I've always been a curious person, and it's served me well because I don't like boredom. I've encountered people who project their boredom onto others, including me, by being negative about *everything*. I realized the more wonder you have, the more self-awareness you have, and the more engaged you are with life. It's a great thing to possess.

TRY IT!

Keep a list of wonders on your phone, on your computer, or in a notebook. The next time you feel bored, take out the list and choose at least one wonder to research and explore. Then put your findings into action.

XENIAL

Instead of looking at each other
like nosy neighbors peeking
from behind our fences in fear,
instead of me seeing you and you
seeing me as *other*, *different*, or *scary*,
we take the leap, invite each other
into our homes, cultures, lives.
Instead of saying, "stay away,"
we both say, "welcome."

Other side: a form that deals with anything on the other side: a neighbor, a window, a wall,
the afterlife, an opposing viewpoint, and more

> **"We are made to tell the world that there are no outsiders. All are welcome: black, white, red, yellow, rich, poor, educated, not educated, male, female, gay, straight, all, all, all."**
>
> —Desmond Tutu

CHARLES SAYS . . .

While attending college, I studied abroad for a semester at Wroxton College in Oxfordshire, England. I also traveled to France, Scotland, and Belgium for short visits. This was my first experience traveling outside the United States, and I encountered many different languages and cultures. Thank goodness people were welcoming to me—a kind Frenchman provided directions when I got lost and a group of Scottish folks invited me to join in while they were celebrating a wedding. During my travels, I heard languages from Flemish to Punjabi and tasted wonderful foods from all over. Although this particular semester was the toughest academic experience I've ever had and my grade point average was the lowest of my college career, I probably learned the most. Sometimes grades don't tell the whole story of one's academic journey.

TRY IT!

Ask your teacher to start a pen pal program with a classroom from another country. Also, look for books in the library or online articles about daily life in other places.

I'm Dr. Affirmative.

First name: <u>Y</u> to the <u>E</u> to the <u>S</u>.

Yes!

Nickname: Amen!

I'm the letters cheering you on,

pushing you forward,

reserving no judgment.

All I ask in return is your best effort.

My friendly competition is named *No*.

Also known as Dr. I Don't Think So.

No has good points every now and again

because it can spur you on to get to

my word, the greatest in all humanity.

If you aim to do well,

not harm anyone,

and accomplish your goals

of being a dynamite,

out-of-sight,

equality-is-right

kind of human—

I'm the word you need

to help you succeed.

M'kay? Ya dig?

Sho nuff.

Persona: written in the voice of the poem's subject

> "yes is a world
> & in this world of
> yes live
> (skillfully curled)
> all worlds"
>
> —E. E. Cummings,
> excerpt from the poem
> "love is a place"

CHARLES SAYS . . .

After my first theatrical performance in college, a friend told me, "I didn't think you were that good." The comment could have led me to decide I wasn't cut out for acting. Instead, I realized that yes, acting was something I wanted to pursue, and I was going to make it happen! If I had listened to all the noes in my life, I wouldn't have become a published author, been part of theatrical tours throughout the country, acted at Walt Disney World, or moved to New York to pursue other opportunities. While that negativity from my friend hurt at the moment, I ultimately ignored it and kept going. Being an actor has been one of the most exhilarating, agonizing, and humbling things I've ever done, and I don't know where I'd be without it. All because I said YES!

TRY IT!

The next time you're offered an opportunity—even (especially!) if it's out of your comfort zone—say yes!

ZEST

Look up, if you want to know enthusiasm—
Sirius and night sky embrace with such enthusiasm!

In autumn, acorns ping, leaves crinkle,
and branches rattle—a merry band of enthusiasm.

Consider zing of horseradish, zest of lemon.
Have you ever tasted such enthusiasm?

The best thing in the morning is to walk into
a coffee-scented room brewing with enthusiasm.

You—nor I—can be unhappy when we give
a hug that's wide and warm with enthusiasm.

Ghazal: an Arabic form that employs
couplets and repetition to tackle
topics of love and loss

> "Zest. Gusto. How rarely one hears these words used. How rarely do we see people living, or for that matter, creating, by them. Yet if I were asked to name the most important items in a writer's make-up, the things that shape his material and rush him along the road to where he wants to go, I could only warn him to look to his zest, see to his gusto."
>
> —Ray Bradbury, *Zen in the Art of Writing: Essays on Creativity*

IRENE SAYS . . .

I tend to be a serious-minded person—which is why I've really worked to cultivate zest in my life. I find the load is lightened when I approach each task, each moment, with good cheer and enthusiasm. I like to surround myself with others who enjoy a similar zest for living, and in fact, it was Charles's enthusiasm for poetry that made me first think we might make good writing partners. I was right! We both share a zest for poetry, as well as a zest for making the world a better place. It's this kind of enthusiasm that has carried us through any difficulties we've experienced while writing, traveling, and performing together.

TRY IT!

Sometimes you have to first imagine zest in order to move forward with a difficult project. Today think about what you want most in the world. Now write what the front page headline would be if your project is wildly successful. For example, when Charles and I first got our book deal, he sent me a card that said, "Latham/Waters Book Sweeps the Nation!" All it takes is a few words to ignite the zest that will help us achieve whatever it is we set out to accomplish.

THE ETYMOLOGY OF PROGRESS

After gathering these words,
we discover
our dictionary is endless!
What makes the world
a zinger
is remembering
we're all in this . . .

Byte: written in 140 characters or less, inspired by
the original character limit for a tweet

AUTHORS' NOTE

"You're imperfect, and you're wired for struggle, but you're worthy of love and belonging."
—Brené Brown

The idea for this book was born on a snowy morning in Grand Rapids, Michigan, in February 2018. Our school visit for the day had been canceled, and we had hours before our flights were scheduled to depart. So we sat across from each other in a restaurant and shared ideas for a second book. The idea that stuck is the one you're holding in your hands.

We've learned a lot about ourselves in the process of writing this book. While we both want to help make the world a better place, we are hyperaware of our limitations. Sometimes the best—and only—thing we can do is to improve ourselves and allow those changes to slowly ripple out into the world. Other times, when we join with others, change can feel like it's happening quickly. We believe it is our job as humans to first be courteous and to at least *try*. We're not experts, and we sure don't know everything. We remain works in progress, even as adults. We're learning every day.

Writing this book has been a great teacher in other ways as well. It forced us to stretch beyond our poetic comfort zones. Each of us naturally gravitates toward writing free verse poems, so challenging ourselves to create form poems was both terrifying and exhilarating. We humbly ask you to look on any mistakes in form as "variations." It can take decades of experience to become masters in some of these forms! We're proud of our efforts, and now that the work is done, we can look back and see how much we've grown as poets. We appreciate how more deeply understanding the constraints of form poetry is already helping us to write stronger free verse poems. And here's something else fun and unexpected: we found new-to-us forms we really *enjoy* writing, such as tricubes and decimas.

We're grateful to all the people in the world working toward change. We're grateful to *you* for sharing your time and heart by reading this book. These poems, these words, are our way of using our voice to help make the world a better place. We hope you'll try some of the prompts included in the book. If you do, we'd love to hear about the changes you're making! You can reach us at our websites: irenelatham.com and charleswaterspoetry.com.

Thank you for joining us!

Irene & Charles

BOOKS, POEMS, AND SPEECH REFERENCED

Auxier, Jonathan. *Sweep: The Story of a Girl and Her Monster*. New York: Amulet Books, 2018.

Bradbury, Ray. *Zen in the Art of Writing: Essays on Creativity*. Santa Barbara, CA: Capra, 1973.

Burgan, Michael, Ed Parker, Kathryn Yingling, and Stephen Crane. *The Red Badge of Courage*. New York: HarperCollins, 1996.

Cummings, E. E. "Love Is a Place." Poetry Society. Accessed July 31, 2019. https://www.poetrysociety.org/psa/poetry/poetry_in_motion/atlas/newyork/lov_is_a_pla/.

DiCamillo, Kate. *The Miraculous Journey of Edward Tulane*. Cambridge, MA: Candlewick, 2006.

Douglass, Frederick. *Narrative of the Life of Frederick Douglass, an American Slave*. Boston: Anti-Slavery Office, 1849.

Erskine, Kathryn. *Mockingbird (Mok'ing-bûrd)*. New York: Philomel Books, 2010.

Frank, Anne, and Otto H. Frank. *The Diary of a Young Girl: The Definitive Edition*. New York: Doubleday, 1995.

Hopkins, Lee Bennett, and Stephen Alcorn. *America at War*. New York: Margaret K. McElderry Books, 2008.

Hosseini, Khaled. *The Kite Runner*. New York: Riverhead Books, 2003.

Kahlo, Frida. *The Diary of Frida Kahlo: An Intimate Self-Portrait*. London: Bloomsbury, 1995.

Kelly, Erin Entrada. *Hello, Universe*. New York: Greenwillow Books, 2017.

Lao-tzu. *Tao Te Ching*. New York: Harper Perennial, 1992.

Larson, Kirby. *Hattie Big Sky*. New York: Delacorte, 2006.

L'Engle, Madeleine. *Walking on Water: Reflections on Faith and Art*. New York: Convergent Books, 2016.

Lester, Julius. *This Strange New Feeling: Three Love Stories from Black History*. New York: Dial Books, 2007.

Lorde, Audre. "The Transformation of Silence into Language and Action." Speech, Lesbian and Literature Panel of the Modern Language Association, Chicago, December 28, 1977. https://electricliterature.com/wp-content/uploads/2017/12/silenceintoaction.pdf.

Marshall, Joseph M., III. *The Lakota Way: Stories and Lessons for Living*. New York: Viking Compass, 2001.

Martin, Bill, Jr., and Michael Sampson. *The Bill Martin Jr. Big Book of Poetry*. New York: Simon and Schuster for Young Readers, 2008.

McCaughrean, Geraldine. *The White Darkness*. New York: HarperTempest, 2007.

Merrell, Billy. *Talking in the Dark: A Poetry Memoir*. New York: Push, 2003.

Montgomery, L. M. *Anne of Green Gables*. New York: Grosset & Dunlap, 1908.

Nye, Naomi Shihab. "Hidden." Vandal Poem of the Day, May 21, 2017. https://poetry.lib.uidaho.edu/index.php/category/naomi-shihab-nye/.

Palacio, R. J. Wonder. New York: Knopf, 2012.

Riordan, Rick. The Battle of the Labyrinth. New York: Hyperion Books for Children, 2008.

Rowling, J. K. The Harry Potter series. New York: Arthur A. Levine Books, 1998–2007.

Ryan, Pam Muñoz. Echo. New York: Scholastic, 2015.

Smith, Philip. Favorite Poems of Childhood. New York: Dover, 1992.

Wiesel, Elie, and Marion Wiesel. The Night Trilogy. New York: Hill and Wang, 2008.

Wong, Janet S. A Suitcase of Seaweed. New York: Margaret K. McElderry Books, 1996.

Woodson, Jacqueline. Brown Girl Dreaming. New York: Nancy Paulsen Books, 2014.

ADDITIONAL RECOMMENDED BOOKS

Acevedo, Elizabeth. The Poet X: A Novel. New York: HarperTeen, 2018.

Alexander, Kwame. The Crossover. Boston: Houghton Mifflin Harcourt, 2014.

———. Rebound. Boston: Houghton Mifflin Harcourt, 2018.

Atkins, Jeannine. Borrowed Names: Poems about Laura Ingalls Wilder, Madam C. J. Walker, Marie Curie, and Their Daughters. New York: Henry Holt, 2010.

———. Finding Wonders: Three Girls Who Changed Science. New York: Atheneum Books for Young Readers, 2016.

Atkins, Laura, Stan Yogi, and Yutaka Houlette. Fred Korematsu Speaks Up. Berkeley, CA: Heyday, 2017.

Bruchac, Joseph, et al. Thanku: Poems of Gratitude. Edited by Miranda Paul. Minneapolis: Millbrook Press, 2019.

Draper, Sharon Mills. Copper Sun. New York: Atheneum Books for Young Readers, 2006.

Engle, Margarita. The Poet Slave of Cuba: A Biography of Juan Francisco Manzano. New York: Henry Holt, 2006.

Greenfield, Eloise. Honey, I Love, and Other Love Poems. New York: Crowell, 1978.

Grimes, Nikki. Garvey's Choice. Honesdale, PA: Wordsong, 2016.

———. One Last Word: Wisdom from the Harlem Renaissance. New York: Bloomsbury, 2017.

Heard, Georgia, ed. *Falling Down the Page*. New York: Roaring Brook, 2009.

Hesse, Karen. *Out of the Dust*. New York: Scholastic, 1997.

Hilton, Marilyn. *Full Cicada Moon*. New York: Dial Books for Young Readers, 2015.

Hoose, Phillip M. *Claudette Colvin: Twice toward Justice*. New York: Melanie Kroupa Books, 2009.

Janeczko, Paul B. *Requiem: Poems of the Terezín Ghetto*. Somerville, MA: Candlewick, 2011.

———. *Worlds Afire*. Cambridge, MA: Candlewick, 2004.

Kennedy, X. J., and Dorothy M. Kennedy. *Knock at a Star: A Childs Introduction to Poetry*. Boston: Little, Brown, 1982.

King, Martin Luther. *Why We Can't Wait*. Boston: Beacon, 2010.

Lai, Thanhha. *Inside Out and Back Again*. New York: Harper, 2011.

Lewis, J. Patrick, ed. *The Poetry of Us: With Favorites from Maya Angelou, Walt Whitman, Gwendolyn Brooks, and More: More Than 200 Poems That Celebrate the People, Places, and Passions of the United States*. Washington, DC: National Geographic, 2018.

Lewis, J. Patrick, and George Ella Lyon. *Voices from the March on Washington: Poems*. Honesdale, PA: WordSong, 2014.

Malcolm X, Alex Haley, and Harold Bloom. *Alex Haley's The Autobiography of Malcolm X*. New York: Bloom's Literary Criticism, 2008.

McCall, Guadalupe Garcia. *Under the Mesquite*. New York: Lee & Low Books, 2011.

Mora, Pat. *Chants*. Houston: Arte Público, 1984.

Morales, Yuyi. *Dreamers*. New York: Neal Porter Books, 2018.

Nagai, Mariko. *Dust of Eden*. Chicago: Albert Whitman, 2014.

Nelson, Marilyn. *Carver, a Life in Poems*. Asheville, NC: Front Street, 2001.

Nelson, Marilyn, and Philippe Lardy. *A Wreath for Emmett Till*. Boston: Houghton Mifflin, 2005.

Nye, Naomi Shihab. *19 Varieties of Gazelle: Poems of the Middle East*. New York: Greenwillow Books, 2002.

Pinkney, Andrea Davis. *The Red Pencil*. New York: Little, Brown, 2014.

Reynolds, Jason. *Long Way Down*. New York: Atheneum, 2017.

Reynolds, Luke. *Fantastic Failures: True Stories of People Who Changed the World by Falling Down First*. Aladdin ed. Hillsboro, OR: Beyond Words, 2018.

Russell, Ching Yeung. *Tofu Quilt*. New York: Lee & Low Books, 2009.

Ryan, Pam Muñoz. *The Dreamer*. New York: Scholastic, 2010.

Sorell, Traci. *We Are Grateful: Otsaliheliga*. Watertown, MA: Charlesbridge, 2018.

Stelson, Caren. *Sachiko: A Nagasaki Bomb Survivor's Story*. Minneapolis: Carolrhoda Books, 2016.

Strickland, Dorothy S., Michael R. Strickland, and John Ward. *Families: Poems Celebrating the African American Experience*. Honesdale, PA: Wordsong, 1994.

Terry, Ellie. *Forget Me Not*. New York: Feiwel and Friends, 2017.

Vardell, Sylvia, and Janet Wong. *The Poetry Friday Anthology for Celebrations: Holiday Poems for the Whole Year in English and Spanish*. Princeton, NJ: Pomelo Books, 2015.

Venkatraman, Padma. *A Time to Dance*. New York: Nancy Paulsen Books, 2014.

Weatherford, Carole Boston. *Schomburg: The Man Who Built a Library*. Somerville, MA: Candlewick, 2017.

———. *Voice of Freedom: Fannie Lou Hamer, Spirit of the Civil Rights Movement*. Somerville, MA: Candlewick, 2015.

Wilson, Kip. *White Rose*. Boston: Houghton Mifflin Harcourt, 2019.

Wolf, Allan. *The Watch That Ends the Night: Voices from the Titanic*. Somerville, MA: Candlewick, 2013.

POETRY RESOURCES

Addonizio, Kim, and Dorianne Laux. *The Poet's Companion: A Guide to the Pleasures of Writing Poetry*. New York: W. W. Norton, 1997.

Alexander, Kwame, and Nina Foxx. *Do the Write Thing: 7 Steps to Publishing Success*. Austin, TX: Manisy Willows Books, 2002.

Digregorio, Charlotte. *Haiku and Senryu: A Simple Guide for All*. Winnetka, IL: Artful Communicators, 2014.

Donegan, Patricia. *Haiku*. Boston: Tuttle, 2003.

Esbensen, Barbara Juster. *A Celebration of Bees: Helping Children Write Poetry*. New York: Holt, 1995.

Fletcher, Ralph J. *Poetry Matters: Writing a Poem from the Inside Out*. New York: HarperTrophy, 2002.

Herrera, Juan Felipe. *Jabberwalking*. Somerville, MA: Candlewick, 2018.

Hewitt, Geof. *Today You Are My Favorite Poet: Writing Poems with Teenagers*. Portsmouth, NH: Heinemann, 1998.

Holbrook, Sara. *Wham! It's a Poetry Jam: Discovering Performance Poetry*. Honesdale, PA: Wordsong, 2002.

Hopkins, Lee Bennett. *Pass the Poetry, Please!* New York: Harper & Row, 1987.

Janeczko, Paul B. *Poetry from A to Z: A Guide for Young Writers*. New York : Simon & Schuster Books for Young Readers, 1994.

———. *Seeing the Blue Between: Advice and Inspiration for Young Poets*. Cambridge, MA: Candlewick, 2002.

Janeczko, Paul B., and Christopher Raschka. *A Kick in the Head*. Cambridge, MA: Candlewick, 2005.

Livingston, Myra Cohn. *Poem-Making: Ways to Begin, Writing Poetry*. New York: HarperCollins, 1991.

Macken, JoAnn Early. *Read, Recite, and Write Concrete Poems*. Edited by Anastasia Suen. New York: Crabtree, 2015.

VanDerwater, Amy Ludwig. *Poems Are Teachers: How Studying Poetry Strengthens Writing in All Genres*. Portsmouth, NH: Heinemann, 2018.

Wolf, Allan, and Tuesday Mourning. *Immersed in Verse: An Informative, Slightly Irreverent & Totally Tremendous Guide to Living the Poet's Life*. New York: Lark Books, 2006.

Wooldridge, Susan. *Poemcrazy: Freeing Your Life with Words*. New York: Clarkson Potter, 1996.

INDEX OF POETIC FORMS

GRATITUDE LIST

1. The 8-1-1 section of the library

2. The following folks, without whom this book would not have been possible: Mehrdokht Amini, Robyn Hood Black, Jill Braithwaite, Robert Lee Brewer, Danielle Carnito, Kathleen Clarke, Andy Cummings, Georgia Heard, Carol Hinz, Paul B. Janeczko, Erica Johnson, Anna Landsverk, Paul Latham, Adam Lerner, Lindsay Matvick, Diane Mayr, Kimberly Morales, Shaina Olmanson, Libby Stille, Rosemary Stimola, Jordyn Taylor, Lois Wallentine, Paula Bantom Waters, and the whole team at Lerner. #proudtobealerner

3. Google Docs, conference calls, Microsoft Word, and the miracle of cellular phones

4. Snow days that allow new ideas to bloom

5. Hashtags. #dictionaryforabetterworld

6. Librarians, educators, and children's book illustrators who are, in fact, magical people

7. Sunday brunches/dinners, because some traditions should never go away

8. You, dear reader. For taking the time to read our book

ADDITIONAL GRATITUDE

Actors Fund, AEA (Actors Equity Association), Al-Anon, Selina Alko, Carlye Allen, Jan Annino, Antioch University Seattle, Steve Aronson, Asheville City Schools Foundation, Jeannine Atkins, Delia Awusi, Linda Baie, Samantha Bailey, Rebecca Baines, Cheryl Bair, Alex Baker, Hillery Baker, Lynn Baker, Matt Baker, Brittany Barnes, Michelle H. Barnes, Stacey Barney, Lucy Dunphy Barsness, Jerri Beck, Ramona Behnke, Doraine Bennett, Paige Bentley-Flannery, Lacresha Berry, Bismarck Cancer Center, Karen Boss, Jean Bradley, Lee Briccetti, Joan Broerman, Kim Broshar, Amy Brown, George Brown, Kent Brown, Jr., Skip Busby, Tammy Busby, the Buttercups (Anna, BrenLeigh, MadiLynn), Ana Canino-Fluit, Carolina Day School, Anthony Centeno, Lori Centeno, the Children's Writer's Guild, Jae Choe, Wroxton College, Valentine Conaty, Ann Marie Corgill, Heather Crowley, Dr. Kirk Curnutt, Damsel, Nicole D'Angelo, Latisha Daring, MaryBeth Davies, Rebecca Davis, Dr. Steven Dawson, Vanessa Dawson, Zoë Detlaf, Kim Doele, Rebecca Kai Dotlich, Ken Dykes Sr., Ken Dykes II, MicaJon Dykes, East Grand Rapids Middle School, Jan Eldredge, Kathy Erskine, Fairleigh Dickinson University, Bob Falls, Dr. Mary L. Farrell, Barbara Fisch, Catherine Flynn, Kathleen Foderaro, Lisa Foderaro, T. J. Foderaro, Joshua France, Jon Freda, Alma Fullerton, Eren T. Gibson, Julie Gribble, Nikki Grimes, Amy Gross, Kristen Guinn, Mary Lee Hahn, David L. Harrison, Leslie Hawkins, Kate Hazel-Busch, Crystal Hendrix, Ruth Hersey, the Highlights Foundation, JuliAnna Hills, Sara Holbrook, Maggie Hollinbeck, Rosi Hollinbeck, Lee Bennett Hopkins, Dr. Jeana Hrepich, Mary Hughs, Kate Jacobs, Mandy James, Jennifer the Original, Britt Chandler Johnson, Cindy Jones, Holly Jones, Travis Jonker, Dr. Christie Kaaland, Angie Karcher, Phoebe Kaufman, Nancy Kelly, Michael Korkis, Ray Kramer, Andrew Latham, Daniel Latham, Eric Latham, Renee LaTulippe, Summer Laurie, Lindsey Leavitt, Kirsten LeClerc, Julius Lester, Bill Levey, Joanne Levy, J. Patrick Lewis, Amanda Lindner, Jo Lloyd, Candice Lucas, Kim Mack-Leveille, Kerry Madden, Kerry Maguire, Malaprops Bookstore/Cafe, Cynthia Malaran (aka D. J. Cherish the Luv), Demosthenes Maratos, Robin Helfritch Maratos, Adam Marcus, Akida Mark, Billeigh Mark, Chris Martin, Isa Martin, Vikki Martin, Anthony Martinez, Melanie McNair, Nancy Mercado, Suzanne Lunden Metzger, Linda Miller, Paige Miller, Monroe #1 BOCES (Board of Cooperative Educational Services), Heidi Mordhorst, Alonso Moreno, Ernesto Moreno, Anthony Morey, Rotem Moscovich, Miranda Musiker, Alison Green Myers, Jamie Campbell Naidoo, Nerdy Book Club, Kenn Nesbitt, Sierra Nimtz, Kellie Otis, Richard Peck, Penn Wood High School, Wendy Petry, Kate Pett, Maureen Phillips, David Piggott, JoAnn Pileggi, Greg Pincus, William Piper, Poets House, Don Pollard, Jane Preston, Denny Price, Zana Price, Sean Qualls, James Rana, Jama Kim Rattigan, Jim Reed, Liz Reed, The Regional Center for College Students with Learning Disabilities, Sheila Renfro, Kristin Rens, Jennifer Rich, Kelly Rivera, Marie Roberts, Michael Romanos, Robin Rosenthal, Ellen Ruffin, SAG-AFTRA (Screen Actors Guild-American Federation of Television and Radio Artists), Laura Purdie Salas, Michael Salinger, Jeremy Sanders, Wendy Sardella, SCBWI (Society of Children's Book Writers and Illustrators), Zoë Scarborough, Gary D. Schmidt, Lisa Schroeder, Colby Sharp, Sarah Shealy, Michael Shenefelt, Laura Shovan, Zestlan Simmons, Margaret Simon, Jamie Simpkins, Marilyn Singer, Kate Skwire, Len Small, Traci Sorell, Mandy Sparks, Spellbound Children's Bookshop, Wendy Stephens, Stimola Literary Studio, Tricia Stohr-Hunt, Peter Sullivan, Sharon Swab, Susan Swagler, Victoria Teerlink, TOFT (Theatre on Film and Tape Archive), Basia Tov, Paige Towler, University School of Milwaukee, Becky Vandenberg, Amy Ludwig VanDerwater, Dr. Sylvia Vardell, Carol Varsalona, George Waters Jr., Keri-Lynn Waters, Suzanne Bartch Waters, Todd Bantom Waters, April Halprin Wayland, Carole Boston Weatherford, Pat Weaver, Michele Weisman, Carol Wilcox, Michele Williams, Kelley Wind, Windermere Preparatory School, Matthew Winner, Elaine Winter, Janet Wong, Dan Woodcock, Sarah Woodcock, Tabatha Yeatts, Paula Zamora-Gonzalez.

And last, but not least, to all our Poetry Friday friends, all our readers, and to the educators, parents, and booksellers who bring poetry to children.

ABOUT THE AUTHORS AND ILLUSTRATOR

IRENE LATHAM lives on a lake in rural Alabama. Winner of the 2016 ILA Lee Bennett Hopkins Promising Poet Award, she is the author of hundreds of poems and nearly twenty current and forthcoming poetry, fiction, and picture books, including *Can I Touch Your Hair? Poems of Race, Mistakes, and Friendship* (with Charles Waters), which was named a Charlotte Huck Honor book and a *Kirkus* Best Book of 2018. Before she was a full-time writer, she earned degrees in social work and finds writing an alternate way to practice meaningful work in the world. She does her best to "live her poem" every single day by laughing, playing the cello, and enjoying nature with her family. Visit her online at irenelatham.com.

CHARLES WATERS is the coauthor (with his poetic forever friend, Irene Latham) of the award-winning book *Can I Touch Your Hair? Poems of Race, Mistakes, and Friendship*. His poems have appeared in many children's poetry anthologies including *Amazing Places*, *The Proper Way to Meet a Hedgehog and Other How-To Poems*, and *One Minute Till Bedtime: 60-Second Poems to Send You Off to Sleep*. As a professional actor, he's toured with multiple theater companies, acted in shows for Walt Disney World, and appeared in various TV shows and commercials. He currently resides in New York City. You can visit his website at www.charleswaterspoetry.com.

MEHRDOKHT AMINI is an Iranian British children's book illustrator who has lived in London since 2004. She has a degree in graphic design from Tehran University and worked for children's magazines and books while still a student. Her picture book, *Golden Domes and Silver Lanterns: A Muslim Book of Colors*, written by Hena Khan, was selected for the 2013 list of Notable Children's Books from the American Library Association. In 2016 *Chicken in the Kitchen* won Best Book at the Children's Africana Book Awards, was named to the White Ravens Honour List, and was nominated for the Kate Greenaway Medal. Amini loves having the opportunity to study different cultures and communities, which gives her a better understanding and appreciation of all people. Visit her website at www.myart2c.com.

For Carol Hinz, Rosemary Stimola, and the late Jane "Tinker" Foderaro, three women who have, and always will, continue to make the world a better place —I.L. & C.W.

To Raha and Madyar —M.A.

Carolrhoda Books®
An imprint of Lerner Publishing Group, Inc.
241 First Avenue North
Minneapolis, MN 55401 USA

For reading levels and more information, look up this title at www.lernerbooks.com.

Charles Waters photo by Kim-Julie Hansen. Irene Latham photo by 205 Photography.

The collage on page 81 includes a partial photograph of gospel and blues singer Aretha Franklin. Known as the Queen of Soul, she released several hit songs including "I Say a Little Prayer," "(You Make Me Feel Like) A Natural Woman," "Chain of Fools," and "Respect." Photo credit: Anthony Barboza/Archive Photos/Getty Images, p. 81 (face detail).

Designed by Mehrdokht Amini and Kimberly Morales.
Main body text set in Bailey Sans ITC Std Book.
Typeface provided by International Typeface Corporation.
The illustrations in this book were created with acrylic, digital painting, collage, and photography.

Library of Congress Cataloging-in-Publication Data

Names: Latham, Irene, author. | Waters, Charles, 1973– author. | Amini, Mehrdokht, illustrator.
Title: Dictionary for a better world : poems, quotes, and anecdotes from A to Z / Irene Latham and Charles Waters ; illustrated by Mehrdokht Amini.
Description: Minneapolis : Carolrhoda Books, [2020] | Audience: Age: 8–12. | Audience: Grade: 4–6.
Identifiers: LCCN 2019000739 (print) | LCCN 2019015860 (ebook) | ISBN 9781541578937 (eb pdf) | ISBN 9781541557758 (lb : alk. paper)
Subjects: LCSH: Conduct of life—Juvenile literature.
Classification: LCC BJ1521 (ebook) | LCC BJ1521 .L38 2019 (print) | DDC 170/.44—dc23
LC record available at https://lccn.loc.gov/2019000739

Manufactured in the United States of America
1-46169-46161-8/5/2019